IT'S TIME TO EAT VEGAN REFRIED BEANS

It's Time to Eat VEGAN REFRIED BEANS

Walter the Educator

Silent King Books
A WhichHead Entertainment Imprint

Copyright © 2024 by Walter the Educator

All rights reserved. No part of this book may be reproduced in any manner whatsoever without written per- mission except in the case of brief quotations embodied in critical articles and reviews.

First Printing, 2024

Disclaimer

This book is a literary work; the story is not about specific persons, locations, situations, and/or circumstances unless mentioned in a historical context. Any resemblance to real persons, locations, situations, and/or circumstances is coincidental. This book is for entertainment and informational purposes only. The author and publisher offer this information without warranties expressed or implied. No matter the grounds, neither the author nor the publisher will be accountable for any losses, injuries, or other damages caused by the reader's use of this book. The use of this book acknowledges an understanding and acceptance of this disclaimer.

It's Time to Eat VEGAN REFRIED BEANS is a collectible early learning book by Walter the Educator suitable for all ages belonging to Walter the Educator's Time to Eat Book Series. Collect more books at WaltertheEducator.com

USE THE EXTRA SPACE TO TAKE NOTES AND DOCUMENT YOUR MEMORIES

VEGAN REFRIED BEANS

It's time to eat, let's grab a spoon,

It's Time to Eat Vegan Refried Beans

The smell of beans fills up the room!

So warm and creamy, soft and brown,

These tasty beans will never let you down.

No need for meat, just spices and care,

A little garlic, a dash of flair.

Mash them up, so smooth and neat,

Vegan refried beans can't be beat!

On tortillas warm, they spread with ease,

Or scoop with chips, as much as you please!

Add avocado, fresh and green,

A perfect pair with our refried beans.

Top them with salsa, mild or hot,

Maybe a sprinkle of cheese, but not!

Vegan choices are kind and smart,

And every bite's a work of art.

It's Time to Eat Vegan Refried Beans

They're good for your tummy, so healthy too,

Packed with protein to power you.

With every bite, you'll feel so strong,

Like you could dance and sing all day long!

Share them with family, share with friends,

The joy of beans just never ends!

A meal so simple, yet full of delight,

Vegan beans make every day bright.

So grab your fork, or use your hand,

A feast of beans is truly grand.

Mix with rice, or eat them plain,

Every mouthful's sunshine after rain.

Eating plants is a kind way to dine,

For you, the earth, and all things fine.

So let's dig in and eat with cheer,

It's Time to Eat

Vegan Refried Beans

Vegan refried beans are the best, my dear!

When your plate is empty, don't feel sad,

You can make more beans, won't that be rad?

Cooking together is oh so fun,

Now let's get started on batch number one!

It's time to clean, let's wash our plate,

Helping out makes dinner great!

With happy hearts and bellies full,

It's Time to Eat Vegan Refried Beans

Vegan beans make life so cool!

ABOUT THE CREATOR

Walter the Educator is one of the pseudonyms for Walter Anderson. Formally educated in Chemistry, Business, and Education, he is an educator, an author, a diverse entrepreneur, and he is the son of a disabled war veteran. "Walter the Educator" shares his time between educating and creating. He holds interests and owns several creative projects that entertain, enlighten, enhance, and educate, hoping to inspire and motivate you. Follow, find new works, and stay up to date with Walter the Educator™

at WaltertheEducator.com

www.ingramcontent.com/pod-product-compliance
Lightning Source LLC
LaVergne TN
LVHW052016060526
838201LV00059B/4051